AF599102

OCEAN LIFE

MARINE MAMMALS & SEABIRDS

by
Claudia Martin

Minneapolis, Minnesota

Credits

Cover and title page, © shanemyersphoto/Adobe Stock, © IakovKalinin/iStock, © georgeclerk/iStock, © elmvilla/iStock, and © Andi Edwards/iStock; 3, © dstephens/iStock; 4–5, © aDam Wildlife/Shutterstock; 4, © Karsten_1/Shutterstock; 5, © wildestanimal/Adobe Stock; 6–7, © Andrew Astbury/Shutterstock; 6, © Collins93/Shutterstock and © synergyfilmsnz/iStock; 7, © Roger Clark ARPS/Shutterstock; 8–9, © Paul R. Sterry/Nature Photographers Ltd/Alamy Stock Photo; 8, © Glenn Bartley, BIA/Minden Pictures/FLPA Images, and © anirbandas08081986/Shutterstock; 9, © John L. Absher/Shutterstock; 10–11, © D Williams Photography/Getty Images; 10, © Bernie Van Der Vyver/Shutterstock; 11, © Karel Gallas/Shutterstock, © Wolf Avni/Shutterstock, and © Dennis Von Linden/Shutterstock; 12–13, © Richard Mittleman/Gon2Foto/Alamy Stock Photo; 12, © FLPA/Alamy Stock Photo and © Brian Lasenby/Shutterstock; 13, © Frank Fichtmueller/Shutterstock; 14–15, © Jeremy Richards/Shutterstock; 14, © David Osborn/Shutterstock and © David Tipling Photo Library/Alamy Stock Photo; 15, © jaroslava V/Shutterstock; 16–17, © Rodrigo Friscione/Cultura Creative (RF)/Alamy Stock Photo; 16, © Ray Hennessy/Shutterstock and © RHIMAGE/Shutterstock; 17, © Don Mammoser/Shutterstock; 18–19, © Simonas Minkevicius/Shutterstock; 18, © Jack Perks/FLPA Images, © Erni/Shutterstock, and © Brian E Kushner/Shutterstock; 19, © Rob Francis/Shutterstock; 20–21, © Enrique Aguirre/Shutterstock; 20, © Nick Pecker/Shutterstock; 21, © Doug Allan/Nature Picture Library/Alamy Stock Photo; 22–23, © Brandon B/Shutterstock; 22, © ChameleonsEye/Shutterstock and © MZPHOTO.CZ/Shutterstock; 23, © Lynsey Allan/Shutterstock; 24–25, © Helmut Corneli/Alamy Stock Photo; 24, © Grobler du Preez/Shutterstock, © Joanne Weston/Shutterstock, © Jeff Stamer/Shutterstock, © zaferkizilkaya/Shutterstock, and © Alexey_Seafarer/iStock; 25, © Chase Dekker/Shutterstock; 26–27, © Frans Lanting/FLPA Images; 26, © Suzi Eszterhas/Minden Pictures/FLPA Images and © Chanonry/Shutterstock; 27, © Kevin Schafer/Minden Pictures/FLPA Images; 28–29, © Hal Brindley/Shutterstock; 28, © Ondrej Prosicky/Shutterstock and © blickwinkel/Frischknecht/Alamy Stock Photo; 29, © Pascal Halder/Shutterstock; 30–31, © Pat Stornebrink/Shutterstock; 30, © Tarpan/Shutterstock and © David Osborn/Shutterstock; 31, © Nicram Sabod/Shutterstock; 32–33, © Christophe Migeon/Biosphoto/FLPA Images; 32, © Wonderly Imaging/Shutterstock and © Tarpan/Shutterstock; 33, © Philip Bird LRPS CPAGB/Shutterstock; 34–35, © FloridaStock/Shutterstock; 34, © AndreAnita/Shutterstock and © Alexey Seafarer/Shutterstock; 35, © Caleb Foster/Shutterstock; 36–37, © Greg Amptman/Shutterstock; 36, © vkilikov/Shutterstock and © Liquid Productions, LLC/Shutterstock; 37, © Jiri Prochazka/Shutterstock; 38–39, © Masa Ushioda/Stephen Frink Collection/Alamy Stock Photo; 38, © Jo Crebbin/Shutterstock and © Top Provide/Adobe Stock; 39, © wildestanimal/Shutterstock; 40–41, © Flip Nicklin/Minden Pictures/FLPA Images; 40, © Tory Kallman/Shutterstock and © Andrew Sutton/Shutterstock; 41, © Andrea Izzotti/Shutterstock; 42, © Shane/Adobe Stock; 43, © Dgwildlife/iStock and © Marko Steffensen/Alamy Stock Photo; 44–45, © dstephens/iStock; 44, © DavidMSchrader/iStock; 45, © Stephen Bishop/iStock; 46–48, © dstephens/iStock; 47, © GlobalP/iStock.

Bearport Publishing Company Product Development Team

Publisher: Jen Jenson; Director of Product Development: Spencer Brinker; Managing Editor: Allison Juda; Editor: Cole Nelson; Associate Editor: Naomi Reich; Associate Editor: Tiana Tran; Art Director: Colin O'Dea; Designer: Kim Jones; Designer: Kayla Eggert; Product Development Specialist: Owen Hamlin

Statement on Usage of Generative Artificial Intelligence

Bearport Publishing remains committed to publishing high-quality nonfiction books. Therefore, we restrict the use of generative AI to ensure accuracy of all text and visual components pertaining to a book's subject. See BearportPublishing.com for details.

Library of Congress Cataloging-in-Publication Data is available at www.loc.gov or upon request from the publisher.

ISBN: 979-8-89232-891-3 (hardcover)
ISBN: 979-8-89232-921-7 (ebook)

For more information, write to Bearport Publishing, 5357 Penn Avenue South, Minneapolis, MN 55419.

Contents

Where It All Began. 4
Seabirds. 6
Plovers and Relatives 8
Herons and Relatives 10
Larids 12
Tubenoses 14
Gannets and Relatives 16
Sea Ducks 18
Puffins and Relatives. 20
Penguins 22
Marine Mammals. 24
Otters. 26
Walruses 28
Seals. 30
Eared Seals 32
Polar Bears 34
Sirenians 36
Whales 38
Dolphins and Porpoises 40
Marine Mammals and Seabirds at Risk 42

Review and Reflect 44
Glossary 46
Read More 47
Learn More Online. 47
Index 48

Where It All Began

Life on Earth began in the ocean about 3.5 billion years ago. Starting with single-celled microbes, life soon became much more complex. Now, the ocean teems with a wide variety of life. Among these life-forms are about 130 species of marine mammals and 310 species of seabirds. Over the course of millions of years, these animals evolved on land before returning to life among the waves.

Life in the Ocean

Marine mammals are found in oceans all around the world. Although they must surface to breathe air, their bodies are uniquely adapted to thrive in the ocean's salty waters. Seabirds have also successfully adapted to ocean life. These birds depend on the sea for food. They spend much of their time on the water.

The Food Web

In the ocean, it's eat and be eaten. Many marine mammals, including polar bears and toothed whales, are apex predators. They eat other animals, such as fish, squid, and crustaceans, while rarely being hunted themselves. While seabirds catch the same types of food as many apex predators, they sometimes also become prey for large marine mammals themselves. Seabird poop fertilizes seagrass and plankton, which become food for fish as well as some marine mammals.

Diving Deep

Orcas, or killer whales, are the largest members of the dolphin family. Scientists used to think there was only one species of orca. However, in 2024, biologists studied genetic, physical, and behavioral data and discovered that Bigg's killer whales and resident killer whales are two different orca species.

Seabirds

About 150 million years ago, birds started to evolve from reptiles called dinosaurs. Like most reptiles, birds lay hard-shelled eggs on land. All birds have wings, a beak, and a covering of feathers. Seabirds find their food beneath the waves, on the ocean surface, or along the shoreline.

Adapted to the Sea

Seabirds have features that help them survive in and around the ocean. Since too much salt is dangerous for birds, many seabirds have glands in their heads to remove the salt they swallow while eating and drinking ocean water. Seabird wings may be flipperlike for swimming beneath the surface or extra-wide for flying great distances over the ocean in search of food. Many seabirds have webbed feet, with skin and tissue joining the toes, making them paddlelike for swimming.

The Atlantic puffin dives as deep as 200 feet (60 m) below the waves in search of fish. It uses short, flipperlike wings as paddles while steering with its webbed feet.

Careful Parents

Seabirds lay fewer eggs than most other birds, many laying only one or two eggs a year. They also spend longer caring for their chicks, with frigatebirds spending the most time—more than 14 months. Seabirds need a different parenting strategy than land birds because life by the stormy sea is dangerous and exhausting. Parents often must travel far in search of food for their chicks.

Blue-footed boobies often have two or three chicks at one time. The eggs hatch four days apart.

SEABIRD RECORDS

Heaviest: Emperor penguin at up to 100 pounds (45 kg)

Largest wingspan: Wandering albatross, up to 11 ft. (3.4 m) wide

Shortest: Least storm petrel, as small as 6 inches (15 cm) tall

Fastest swimmer: Gentoo penguin, up to 22 miles per hour (35 kph)

Longest living: Laysan albatross, possibly more than 66 years

DID YOU KNOW? An Arctic tern flies about 1.5 million miles (2.4 million km) in its life. It goes between Arctic coasts and Antarctica during different times of year.

Plovers and Relatives

Plovers and their relatives are called shorebirds. They often live on beaches and mudflats, where they search for invertebrates in the sand or mud. These small- to medium-sized birds have long legs for wading through the shallows. Many of them also have long beaks to probe for food.

The wrybill is a species of plover that lives along the coasts of New Zealand, flying inland to nest beside rivers during springtime.

Oystercatchers

Oystercatchers have large orange-and-red beaks that they use for opening the shells of mollusks such as oysters, mussels, and limpets. These birds usually attack their prey when the tide is going out, before the invertebrates have fully closed their shells after feeding. Oystercatchers also dig in soft sand and mud to find worms.

The Magellanic oystercatcher has yellow eyes, surrounded by a ring of yellow skin.

BLACK-NECKED STILT

Length: Up to 16 in. (41 cm)

Range: Coastal shorelines from the United States to Argentina

Habitat: Coasts and wetlands

Diet: Small invertebrates, fish, and tadpoles

Conservation: Population shrinking in some regions due to habitat loss

DID YOU KNOW? Plovers get their name from the Latin word *pluvia,* meaning rain. People used to think they formed flocks when it was about to rain.

The wrybill's beak bends to the right, making it the only bird in the world with a beak that bends to one side. This shape helps the bird reach invertebrates hiding beneath rocks.

Avocets and Stilts

These waders have long, thin legs and beaks, as well as striking plumage, usually featuring black and white patches. Avocets feed by sweeping their upturned beaks from side to side through shallow water or across the surface of mud, looking for shrimp, insects, and worms. Stilts usually hunt by sight alone, using their straight beaks to jab into the water to seize small invertebrates and fish.

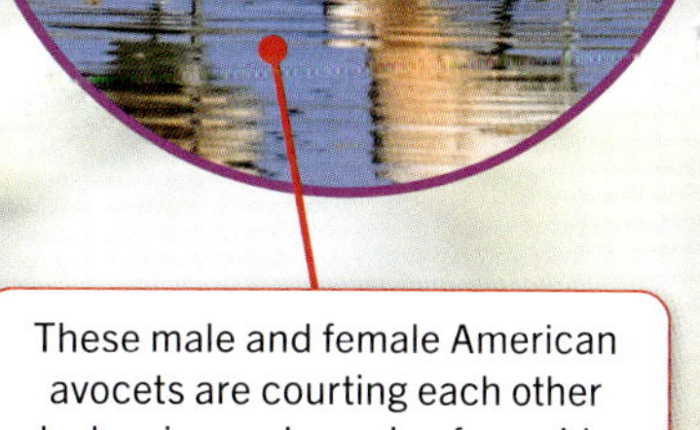

These male and female American avocets are courting each other by bowing and swaying from side to side. Soon, the pair will build a nest of twigs close to the water.

Gray and white plumage offers camouflage on stony or sandy shores and riverbeds.

Herons and Relatives

Herons, spoonbills, and hammerkops are wading birds with long legs and beaks. They live around the edges of oceans or fresh water. These birds have four toes, with three pointing forward and one backward. The toes are long and have webbing between them to prevent the birds from sinking into mud.

The Goliath Heron

The largest heron, the goliath, stands up to 5 ft. (1.5 m) tall and has a wingspan of up to 7.5 ft. (2.3 m). It is found around coral reefs, mangrove forests, lakes, and swamps in Africa. While hunting, the goliath usually stands completely still in shallow water. When a fish swims past, the bird spears it with an open beak, then swallows it whole.

The plumage of the goliath heron's head and neck is chestnut-colored.

The roseate spoonbill's feathers turn pink from eating crustaceans that consume lots of red algae.

DID YOU KNOW? A spoonbill's nostrils are at the base of its beak, close to its eyes. This lets it breathe when its beak is underwater while hunting.

The Hammerkop

This African bird hunts for fish, frogs, and shrimp in shallow water. It is found around salt water as well as fresh water. The hammerkop is an unusual wader because it spends a lot of time building giant stick nests in trees, often above water. Its nests can reach 6 ft. (1.8 m) wide.

Hammerkops build several nests every year.

Hammerkops often stand on top of one another, perhaps as a way to form bonds within their flock.

To catch invertebrates, the bird swings its flat, spoon-shaped beak from side to side while wading through shallow water.

The roseate spoonbill lives around coasts and fresh water in North and South America.

TRICOLORED HERON

Length: Up to 30 in. (76 cm)

Range: Coastal shorelines from the northeastern United States to Brazil

Habitat: Mangrove forests, bays, and coastal marshes

Diet: Fish, amphibians, crustaceans, and insects

Conservation: Not at risk

Larids

Gulls, skimmers, and skuas are members of the Lari suborder. They are large seabirds that pluck fish from the ocean's surface. These bold birds are also known to attack other birds to snatch food and steal eggs. Some have adapted to living inland and taking food wherever they find it, including from landfills.

Kleptoparasitism

Kleptoparasitism is when an animal eats the food that another animal has caught. Most gulls and skuas steal from other seabirds, either occasionally or as a main feeding method. A kleptoparasitic bird will use its strength, size, and sharp beak to attack another bird that has food. When the other bird drops the food, the kleptoparasitic bird will steal it. Gulls do not limit themselves to stealing from other birds. Some swoop on humans' food, too!

A laughing gull is trying to force a white ibis to drop its fish.

Skimmers

Skimmers have an unusual beak shape, with a lower jaw that is longer than the upper. This allows them to hunt by flying low over the water with their beak slightly open. As the beak skims along the water's surface, the bird snatches up any small fish that aren't quick enough to dart away.

Measuring up to 20 in. (50 cm) long, the black skimmer hunts in the coastal waters of North and South America, as well as in rivers and lakes.

GREAT SKUA

Length: Up to 23 in. (58 cm)

Range: Northern Atlantic Ocean

Habitat: Open ocean; nests on coasts and islands

Diet: Fish, birds, eggs, rodents, rabbits, and dead animals

Conservation: Not at risk

DID YOU KNOW? A herring gull was spotted using pieces of bread as bait to catch goldfish in a pond in Paris, France.

Tubenoses

Albatross, petrels, and shearwaters are tubenoses, named for the shape of their beaks. These seabirds have three webbed toes for paddling in the water, and many have wide wings for flying great distances over the ocean in search of fish. They nest in large groups called colonies, often on remote islands.

Tube Nostrils

Tubenoses have large tube-shaped nostrils on the tops or sides of their beaks. These nostrils give the birds a very good sense of smell, which they use for finding prey. Tubenose beaks are covered in horny plates and hooked at the tip. Like other seabirds, tubenoses have a salt gland above their eyes. This gets rid of the salt they take in while swimming and eating. The gland releases salty liquid, which exits through the nostrils and drips down a groove in the beak.

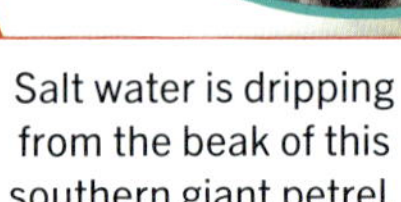

Salt water is dripping from the beak of this southern giant petrel.

Petrels fly low over the waves, their feet just touching the surface. This makes it look as if they are walking on water. Petrels are named after St. Peter, who was said to walk on water.

Diving Petrels

Most tubenoses pluck prey from the surface of the water, but diving petrels go down as deep as 270 ft. (80 m) underwater to snap up food. When diving, they fold their wings halfway in order to use them as paddles. Unlike their relatives, diving petrels are small with short wings, so they feed close to the shore instead of making long flights.

DID YOU KNOW? The wandering albatross has the largest wingspan of any bird, reaching 11.5 ft. (3.5 m) wide.

WANDERING ALBATROSS
Length: Up to 53 in. (135 cm)
Range: Antarctic Ocean and southern Atlantic, Indian, and Pacific Oceans
Habitat: Open ocean; nests on islands
Diet: Squid, fish, crustaceans, and waste from ships
Conservation: Population shrinking due to tangling in fishing lines and pollution
This pillar-like nest is built from mud.
The black-browed albatross has smaller nostril tubes than some of its relatives.
Black-browed albatross lay only one egg per year. The chick stays in the nest for around four months.

Gannets and Relatives

Gannets, boobies, cormorants, and frigatebirds are members of the Suliformes order. They are medium to large birds with hooked or cone-shaped beaks. All four of their toes are fully webbed. Frigatebirds snatch fish from the surface of the water, while the other birds are expert underwater divers.

Diving Styles

Cormorants dive down from the water's surface, swimming to depths of 150 ft. (46 m) using their strong, webbed feet. Gannets and boobies are plunge divers, dropping into the water from high in the sky. For this reason, they do not have nostrils on the outside of their beaks, which would fill with water as they crashed into the ocean. Instead, they breathe through their mouths. They also have air sacs in their faces and chests to act as a cushion for the impact with the water.

The northern gannet plunge-dives from heights of up to 70 ft. (21 m).

RED-FOOTED BOOBY

Length: Up to 30 in. (76 cm)

Range: Tropical Atlantic, Indian, and Pacific Oceans

Habitat: Open ocean; nests on islands

Diet: Small fish and squid

Conservation: Not at risk

Frigatebirds

There are five species of frigatebirds. They all live around tropical and subtropical oceans. During mating season, frigatebirds cluster on remote islands in large colonies. The males of all species have bright red throat pouches. To attract females, the males inflate these pouches, lift their heads, and open and shake their wings.

DID YOU KNOW? The name *booby* comes from the Spanish slang word *bobo*, meaning silly.

Sea Ducks

Although most people think of ducks as freshwater birds, more than 20 species spend part of the year in coastal seas. Ducks have broad, rounded bodies that float easily as well as webbed feet and strong legs for paddling.

Diving Ducks

Many freshwater ducks feed by tipping themselves into shallow water, pointing toward the bottom with their tails in the air. These dabbling ducks feed mostly on water plants. In contrast, most sea ducks are divers, able to swim deep to the ocean floor in order to prey on water creatures. Diving ducks usually have bigger feet that are set farther back on their bodies than dabblers, making them waddle awkwardly on land.

The common eider swallows mussels whole. The shells are crushed in a muscly part of its stomach called the gizzard.

The black scoter spends its winters along the coasts of the northern Atlantic Ocean.

The red-breasted merganser hunts for small fish.

Useful Beaks

Like all birds, ducks do not have teeth, so they swallow their food whole. Their strong beaks and jaws allow them to tear off plants or grapple with prey. A duck's beak shape is suited to its diet. Scoter ducks have large, broad beaks for poking in mud and grasping hard-shelled crustaceans and mollusks. The mergansers have jagged edges to their long, thin beaks, which helps them grasp their slippery fishy prey.

SPECTACLED EIDER

Length: Up to 22 in. (56 cm)

Range: Arctic and northern Pacific Oceans

Habitat: Open ocean and coastal waters; nests on wetlands

Diet: Mollusks, crustaceans, insects, grasses, and berries

Conservation: Population shrinking due to climate change

DID YOU KNOW? In the past, eider ducks were hunted for the layer of very soft, thick down feathers next to their skin, which were used to make eiderdown quilts.

Puffins and Relatives

Both male and female tufted puffins grow long tufts of feathers as summer approaches.

Puffins are members of the auk family, along with guillemots and auklets. These seabirds are high-speed underwater divers, with wings that work best as paddles. In the air, they have to flap their short wings very quickly to stay aloft. On land, they are clumsy walkers, with an upright penguin-like posture.

Egg Laying

Birds in the auk family spend most of their lives far out to sea, but they gather in colonies along the coast during mating season. They often return to the same mate year after year, having just one to two eggs at a time. Most species nest on cliff ledges or in rock clefts, where their eggs stay out of reach of predators.

The thick-billed murre lays its egg on a cliff ledge. This egg is pointed at one end, which makes it roll in a circle rather than off the ledge if the egg starts to move.

PARAKEET AUKLET

Length: Up to 10 in. (25 cm)

Range: Northern Pacific Ocean

Habitat: Open ocean; nests on rocky islands

Diet: Jellyfish, crustaceans, and small fish

Conservation: Population shrinking on some islands due to accidental introduction of rats

DID YOU KNOW? By around 1852, the great auk had been driven to extinction by human hunters who wanted its feathers, eggs, and meat.

Deft Divers

Auks need to move quickly underwater to capture the speedy fish they eat. The birds must hold their breath throughout a dive, so they angle their streamlined bodies to descend to their desired depth as swiftly as possible. They use up-and-down wing strokes to change direction as they pursue their prey.

The common guillemot can dive to depths of 490 ft. (150 m).

Penguins

A penguin's small wings are shaped like a dolphin's flippers. Though great for swimming, these wings cannot lift the penguin into the air at all. These seabirds spend three-quarters of their lives swimming in the ocean, with most species living in the cold waters of the southern hemisphere. They have a thick layer of fat called blubber and waterproof feathers that help keep them warm.

Hunters

Penguins dive for fish, squid, and krill. The largest species can dive as deep as 1,800 ft. (550 m) for up to 22 minutes. Smaller species cannot swim as fast or hold their breath for as long. They find their food near the surface. All penguins catch prey in their beaks and swallow it whole as they swim.

When the gentoo penguin is swimming, its movements look similar to a bird flying through the air.

The world's largest penguin colony is on Zavodovskiy Island, in the Southern Ocean. It is home to more than one million chinstrap and macaroni penguins.

Getting Together

Penguins are sociable birds. They hunt, sleep, and nest with other penguins. Many species come to land only to mate, when they gather in large, loud colonies. Penguins often return to the same mate year after year. In most species, males and females share the responsibility of caring for eggs and young chicks.

SOUTHERN ROCKHOPPER PENGUIN

Height: Up to 22 in. (56 cm)

Range: Southern Atlantic, Indian, and Pacific Oceans

Habitat: Open ocean; nests on rocky islands and coasts

Diet: Krill, fish, squid, and octopuses

Conservation: Population shrinking due to climate change, overfishing, and oil spills

DID YOU KNOW? The Galápagos penguin is the only penguin that does not live in the southern hemisphere, as its island home sits on the equator.

Marine Mammals

About 130 species of mammals spend all or part of their lives in the ocean. Like all other mammals, these animals need to breathe air, so they come to the surface regularly. All female mammals feed their young milk.

Family Life

All marine mammals give birth to live young. Apart from polar bears, which can give birth to up to three cubs at once, marine mammals have just one baby at a time. They look after their young for several months or even years. From the songs of whales to the barks of sea lions, all marine mammals make sounds to communicate with one another.

A Cape fur seal feeds her pup milk from her body.

Groups of Marine Mammals

Marine mammals are not all closely related to one another. They belong to different scientific groups with varying bodies and lifestyles.

CETACEANS	SIRENIANS	PINNIPEDS	MARINE FISSIPEDS
CHARACTERISTICS: These mammals never leave the water. They have a streamlined body and two limbs that are flippers.	**CHARACTERISTICS:** Like cetaceans, sirenians never leave the water. They have a rounded body and two limbs that are flippers.	**CHARACTERISTICS:** These meat-eaters spend part of their lives on land. They have four flipper-like limbs, some of which have claws.	**CHARACTERISTICS:** These mammals spend more time on land than other marine mammals. They go underwater mainly to hunt for food. Sea otters even give birth underwater.
SPECIES: Around 90 whales, dolphins, and porpoises	**SPECIES:** Three manatees and one dugong	**SPECIES:** 33 sea lions, walruses, and seals	**SPECIES:** Polar bears and 13 otter species
 Minke whale	 West Indian manatee	 Mediterranean monk seal	 Polar bear

MARINE MAMMAL RECORDS

Heaviest and longest: Blue whale at up to 330,000 lb. (150,000 kg) and 110 ft. (34 m) long

Heaviest and longest pinniped: Southern elephant seal, up to 11,000 lb. (5,000 kg) and 22 ft. (7 m) long

Shortest: Marine otter, as small as 34 in. (86 cm) long

Fastest swimmer: Common dolphin, up to 40 mph (64 kph)

Longest living: Bowhead whale, possibly up to 200 years

DID YOU KNOW? All mammals grow hair at some point in their lives, but most whales and dolphins are nearly hairless as adults.

Otters

There are 13 species of otters, all of which are meat-eating mammals that spend part or most of their lives in water. Two species, sea and marine otters, live only in salt water, while the Eurasian otter moves between coastal oceans and rivers. All the other otters live around fresh water.

Sea otters rest together in large groups called rafts, sometimes holding one another's paws.

Sea Otter

Unlike other marine mammals, otters do not have blubber. Their slim bodies are covered in thick fur to keep them warm. The sea otter lives in coastal waters of the northern and eastern Pacific Ocean. Its back paws are wide and webbed for paddling, while the smaller front paws have sharp claws for catching prey. The sea otter dives to the seafloor in search of sea urchins, mollusks, crustaceans, and fish. The clever otter then uses rocks to break open the tough shells of their prey.

This sea otter is cracking open a clam on the side of a boat.

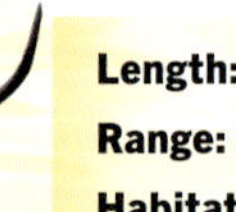

EURASIAN OTTER

Length: Up to 3 ft. (1 m)

Range: Rivers and coasts of Europe, North Africa, and Asia

Habitat: Rivers, lakes, and coastal oceans with fresh water nearby for washing off salt

Diet: Fish, crustaceans, insects, and birds

Conservation: Population shrinking in some regions due to habitat loss and pollution

Marine Otter

Unlike the sea otter, which spends nearly all its life in the ocean, the marine otter spends a lot of time on rocky beaches. It is found along the western coast of South America, where it hunts for crabs, mollusks, shrimps, and fish. Like the sea otter, the marine otter is endangered due to harm from oil spills and other pollution. In the past, it was hunted for its fur.

DID YOU KNOW? The sea otter has the thickest fur of any animal, with up to one million hairs per square inch (about 150,000 hairs per square cm).

Walruses

Although closely related to seals, walruses are the only species in their family. A walrus has four flippers, long tusks, and whiskers. Its thick blubber keeps it warm in the freezing temperatures of the far north. Blubber also makes the walrus extremely heavy, with some animals weighing as much as 3,700 lb. (1,700 kg).

Whiskers

Walruses have mats of bristly whiskers, called vibrissae, on their snouts. These hairs are linked to nerves, making them extremely sensitive. Walruses use their whiskers to feel movement in the water and find prey on the muddy, dark seabed.

This walrus calf (*left*) and its mother each have up to 700 whiskers. A calf will stay with its mother for up to five years.

Outside the mating season, hundreds of walruses crowd together in single-sex groups on beaches.

Tusks

Both male and female walruses have tusks, but a male's tusks are slightly longer, reaching up to 3 ft. (1 m). Tusks are the walrus's canine teeth, which are the pointed, fanglike teeth of all mammals. Tusks are used to climb onto slippery sea ice and for making breathing holes. Male walruses also use their tusks to fight other males when defending their mates.

During mating season, male walruses fight frequently. The largest males with the biggest tusks usually win.

WALRUS

Length: Up to 11.8 ft. (3.6 m)

Range: Coastal Arctic Ocean and far northern Atlantic and Pacific Oceans

Habitat: Sea ice, shallow coastal ocean, and rocky beaches

Diet: Clams and other bivalves, worms, shrimp, and crabs

Conservation: Population at risk from global warming and hunting

DID YOU KNOW? Due to its great size, the walrus has only two non-human predators—polar bears and orcas. It can sometimes defend itself successfully against either.

Seals

Living for up to 40 years, the harbor seal is found in coastal waters of the northern Atlantic and Pacific Oceans.

There are 19 species of true seals. All seals have a streamlined body suited to swimming and deep diving, with two large back flippers for paddling and two smaller, clawed front flippers for steering. Since their back flippers cannot be pulled under the body for walking, true seals have to wriggle along on land.

Fast Parenting

True seals are so suited to life in the ocean that they rarely go ashore. However, they do come onto land or sea ice to give birth. A mother seal gives birth to only one pup at a time. She then feeds the baby extremely high-fat milk for just a few days or weeks, depending on the species, before returning to the sea to hunt so she can survive. The pup lives off the fat it has built up until it has learned to hunt for itself.

A young Weddell seal yelps to tell its mother it is hungry for milk.

A seal's eyes can see well both above and below the water. When diving, a thin membrane, or see-through eyelid, covers the eyeball for protection.

Elephant Seals

The largest seal is the southern elephant seal. Males reach up to 21 ft. (6.4 m) long. Elephant seals are named for the males' large snouts, which look a little like an elephant's trunk. The hollow, muscly snout acts a bit like a horn, making the male's roars even louder.

The male elephant seal roars to warn away other males who might try to compete for females.

GRAY SEAL

Length: Up to 10.8 ft. (3.3 m)

Range: Coastal northern Atlantic Ocean

Habitat: Coastal ocean, rocks, islands, and beaches

Diet: Fish, octopuses, and lobsters

Conservation: Population growing since bans on hunting

DID YOU KNOW? The Weddell seal lives farther south than any other mammal, since it lives on the sea ice surrounding Antarctica.

Eared Seals

Sea lions and fur seals are known as eared seals because, unlike true seals, the openings to their ears are covered by ear flaps. There are six species of sea lions and nine species of fur seals. They can be found in all the world's oceans except the Arctic and northern Atlantic.

Walking on All Fours

Unlike true seals, which have small front paws, eared seals have large front flippers. Their back flippers can be turned forward, allowing eared seals to walk on all fours. This makes them much more agile when on land, where they spend more of their time than true seals. Large and noisy groups of these creatures, called rookeries, can be seen on beaches. Female eared seals spend longer caring for their pups than true seals—up to one year. While mothers go hunting, pups often gather together to play.

These female California sea lions have gathered underwater, close to their rookery.

The endangered Australian sea lion lives on the beaches and in the coastal waters around southwestern Australia.

NORTHERN FUR SEAL

Length: Up to 7 ft. (2 m)

Range: Coastal northern Pacific Ocean

Habitat: Ocean and beaches

Diet: Fish and squid

Conservation: Population at risk from global warming, pollution, and tangling in nets

DID YOU KNOW? Eared seals are known for the loud barking and honking calls they make to one another. The seals also make trumpet sounds when they spot a predator.

Hair or Fur

Sea lions have short, rough hair, but fur seals have soft fur. Their fur includes coarse guard hairs and thicker, softer underfur. During the eighteenth and nineteenth centuries, fur seals were widely hunted for their fur. Some species, including the Cape, northern, and Guadalupe fur seals, were hunted almost to extinction. Since hunting has been banned or limited by many countries, most species have slowly recovered.

Polar Bears

The polar bear lives in and around the Arctic Ocean, where it hunts for its favorite food—seals. These bears are born on land but spend most of their lives on the ice floating in the ocean. When they dive into the cold water, thick body fat and fur keep them warm.

Born in a Den

Mating season for polar bears is in the spring. During the autumn, a female polar bear digs a den in the snow, then climbs inside to rest. Snow soon covers the entrance, making it warm inside. During the winter, mothers give birth in their dens, often to two cubs at a time. When spring comes, the family leaves the den and heads for sea ice, where the mother hunts for food for the whole family.

Cubs stay with their mother until they are about two and a half years old.

Hunting Seals

Polar bears usually wait around for their meals after having used their powerful sense of smell to find a seal breathing hole. When a seal pops up to breathe, the bear drags it out with a clawed paw. Sometimes, polar bears spot seals resting on ice. They creep up to them slowly before rushing in for a deadly attack.

Polar bears eat as many seals as possible from winter to summer, storing up energy for the late summer and autumn, when the sea ice melts and it becomes more difficult to hunt.

DID YOU KNOW? The longest known underwater dive by a polar bear lasted 3 minutes and 10 seconds.

POLAR BEAR

Length: Up to 10 ft. (3 m)

Range: The coastal Arctic Ocean and surrounding land

Habitat: Sea ice, ocean, and land when sea ice melts in late summer to autumn

Diet: Ringed, bearded, and other seals, plus bird eggs and dead walruses and whales

Conservation: Population at risk due to global warming

Sirenians

The West Indian manatee lives on the warm eastern coast of North and South America, from the United States to Brazil, often swimming inland up rivers.

Sirenians are an order of mammals that includes manatees and the dugong. They live in warm and shallow water, ranging from coastal seas to swamps and rivers. These animals are mostly plant-eaters, using their strong lips to rip off leaves and stems. They have heavy bones and rounded bodies, making them slow swimmers.

The Dugong

The dugong, which reaches 10 ft. (3 m) long and lives for up to 70 years, is one of the four species of sirenians. It lives in warm coastal waters of the Indian and Pacific Oceans. Like all sirenians, it has no dorsal fin or back limbs, but it has flipper-like front limbs. Unlike its cousin the manatee, its snout is downturned, which makes it easier for the creature to feed on bottom-growing seagrass. It has peglike teeth for grinding plants.

The dugong is most easily distinguishable from the manatee by its fluked tail, similar to that of a dolphin.

Manatees

There are three species of manatees. West Indian and African manatees live in both coastal waters and nearby rivers and wetlands. The Amazonian manatee lives only in the Amazon River in South America. Adult male manatees usually swim alone, while mothers and their calves usually stay together for one to two years. Adults also form groups during the mating season.

This West Indian manatee calf is drinking milk from its mother. Mothers and calves squeak to communicate with each other.

AFRICAN MANATEE

Length: Up to 15 ft. (4.6 m)

Range: Tropical coasts of western Africa

Habitat: Shallow coastal ocean, rivers, and lakes

Diet: Mostly plants, including mangrove leaves and seagrass, as well as bivalves

Conservation: Population shrinking due to hunting and habitat loss

DID YOU KNOW? The closest living relatives of sirenians are elephants, which are also plant-eating mammals with thick skin.

Whales

Along with dolphins and porpoises, whales belong to the group of marine mammals called cetaceans. Cetaceans power through the water with their tails, steering with their two flippers. They spend their whole lives in the water but come to the surface to breathe air through the blowholes on top of their heads.

Baleen

There are around 15 species of baleen whales. Baleen whales are named for the plates of bristly baleen in their mouths. Baleen is made of keratin, the same tough material that makes human nails. When it feeds, a baleen whale takes in a mouthful of water, either by lunge-feeding (taking a huge gulp) or skim-feeding (swimming with an open mouth). The water is then released through the baleen plates, which trap small prey inside the mouth.

This gray whale is showing its baleen plate. Gray whales are skim-feeders, scooping up sand, water, and tiny crustaceans as they swim over the seafloor.

Toothed Whales

Sperm whales, beaked whales, and white whales all have teeth for catching prey. While baleen whales have two blowholes, toothed whales have just one. Scientists also include dolphins and porpoises in the toothed whale group, though these animals are usually smaller.

The beluga whale dives in search of fish. Since its teeth are small and blunt, it has to swallow prey whole.

SOUTHERN RIGHT WHALE

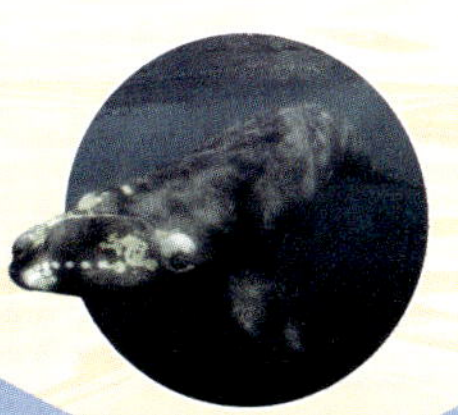

Length: Up to 56 ft. (17 m)

Range: Antarctic Ocean in summer; southern Atlantic, Indian, and Pacific Oceans in winter

Habitat: Open ocean in summer; coastlines in winter

Diet: Zooplankton and krill

Conservation: Endangered after centuries of hunting by humans

Barnacles often attach themselves to a humpback whale's skin.

Humpback flippers have knobs called tubercles. These are enlarged hair follicles, or roots from which hairs grow.

The humpback whale often leaps partway out of the water, in an activity called breaching.

DID YOU KNOW? The blue whale is the largest animal that ever lived and can eat 6 tons (5.4 t) of krill per day. However, it cannot swallow anything bigger than a beach ball.

Dolphins and Porpoises

Dolphins are small toothed whales, with streamlined bodies for fast swimming and cone-shaped teeth for grasping prey. To communicate with one another, dolphins make a wide range of sounds, from clicks to whistles. About 36 species of dolphins live in the oceans, with another 5 or 6 species living in rivers.

Living in a Pod

Dolphins are very sociable, living in pods that differ in size from species to species. A small pod may contain just a mother and her calves. Where there is plenty of prey, family pods join together in groups with hundreds or even thousands of dolphins. Dolphins show strong bonds between friends and relatives. They often help weaker members of their pod, staying beside injured group members or helping them to the surface to breathe.

At up to 32 ft. (10 m) long, orcas are the largest dolphins. They are sometimes called killer whales. Females travel in family pods led by the oldest member.

Porpoises

Porpoises are closely related to dolphins, but they do not have beaks and have spade-shaped teeth. There are seven species of porpoises, including the tiniest cetacean, the vaquita, which is just 5 ft. (1.5 m) long.

Since the finless porpoise lives in coastal waters, it is particularly at risk from human behavior.

STRIPED DOLPHIN

Length: Up to 9 ft. (3 m)

Range: Temperate to tropical Atlantic, Indian, and Pacific Oceans

Habitat: Usually deep oceans away from coasts

Diet: Fish, squid, octopuses, krill, and other crustaceans

Conservation: Population shrinking due to tangling in nets, collisions with boats, and pollution

DID YOU KNOW? The smallest dolphin is the critically endangered Maui's dolphin, which lives off the coast of New Zealand and reaches 5.3 ft. (1.6 m) long.

Marine Mammals and Seabirds at Risk

Marine mammals and seabirds have thrived in oceans for millions of years, but many human activities are making life harder for these animals. Pollution and climate change damage their habitats. These ocean animals can be accidentally injured or killed by fishing gear and boats. Many marine mammals and seabirds have become endangered or threatened. If they are not protected, they could become extinct.

Scientists and researchers are learning more about these endangered animals in order to help them. Some researchers attach satellite tracking tags to marine animals and use satellites and research ships to gather data on the creatures' health and movement. Others use underwater drones and remote-controlled robots to capture images that allow scientists to monitor known species and discover new ones. The data from these technologies will allow scientists to learn more about how marine creatures survive and how to protect them.

Scientists use remote-controlled robots to explore parts of the ocean too dangerous or difficult for humans to visit.

Vaquitas

Vaquitas, a kind of porpoise, are critically endangered. Recent estimates suggest there may be fewer than 20 remaining in the world. In an attempt to save the species, local governments established a vaquita refuge in the Gulf of California, where commercial fishing is banned. Conservation groups work to remove illegal gill nets, a type of fishing gear that can be deadly to vaquitas and other marine animals.

Review and Reflect

Now that you've read about marine mammals and seabirds, let's review what you've learned. Use the following questions to reflect on your newfound knowledge and integrate it with what you already knew.

Check for Understanding

1. Describe two ways seabirds are different from other birds. *(See p. 6)*
2. How do oystercatchers catch their prey? What do they tend to eat? *(See p. 8)*
3. In what ways are spoonbills' beaks adapted to help them search for prey? *(See pp. 10–11)*
4. What is kleptoparasitism? Describe an example of this behavior. *(See pp. 12–13)*
5. How do tubenoses avoid taking in too much salt from their habitats? *(See p. 14)*
6. Why do different sea ducks have different kinds of beaks? What is the shape of a scoter duck's beak? *(See pp. 18–19)*
7. How do birds in the auk family ensure their eggs stay safe? *(See p. 20)*
8. What features does a penguin have to keep warm in the southern hemisphere? *(See p. 22)*
9. Name the different groups of marine mammals. Which groups never leave water? *(See p. 24)*
10. How do sea otters get to the meat of their tough-shelled prey? *(See p. 26)*
11. What are a walrus's whiskers called? Why are they so important? *(See p. 28)*
12. How are seals able to see underwater? *(See p. 30)*
13. What is the main difference between sea lions and fur seals? *(See p. 33)*
14. How does a polar bear hunt? Why is it important for them to catch as many seals as possible from winter to summer? *(See p. 34)*
15. What are the benefits of dolphins living in a pod? *(See pp. 40–41)*

Making Connections

1. Seabirds spend a lot of time taking care of their young. Explain why it is so important for them to do this, and list some of the ways different seabirds care for their chicks.

2. List three ways different seabirds catch their prey, and describe how the body parts the birds have influenced these methods.

3. What traits do marine mammals in the fissipeds group have? How do these traits separate them from other marine mammals?

4. How are sea otters and marine otters different from each other? How are they similar?

5. Seals are a noisy bunch. What are some of the different ways they communicate with one another? What are the different purposes of the sounds they make?

In Your Own Words

1. Seabirds come in all different shapes and sizes. What do you think are some advantages and disadvantages of being a large seabird? What about a small one?

2. Think of a common bird on land. Which seabird traits would make it better suited to living along a coast or on the ocean?

3. Several seabirds don't have the ability to fly. Do you think this is an advantage or a disadvantage? Why do you think they evolved in this way?

4. Why do you think so many marine mammals work in groups? If you lived in the ocean, would you want others around you or would you prefer to be on your own?

5. Many marine species are at risk of extinction. What do you think would happen if all these animals disappeared from Earth? What are some ways these animals can be protected?

Glossary

algae simple plants and plantlike chromists that usually live in and around water

bivalves soft-bodied invertebrates that live in a hinged two-part shell

camouflage the way the color and shape of an animal make it blend into its habitat

crustaceans arthropods with two pairs of antennae on their heads

dorsal fin the fin on the back of a fish or a cetacean

endangered likely to become extinct in the near future

evolve to change and adapt gradually over time

gland a body part that makes a substance for use in the body or for release

global warming rising world temperatures caused mainly by human activities

habitat the natural home of an animal, plant, or other living thing

invertebrate an animal without a backbone, such as a crab, squid, or insect

marine found in the ocean

mudflat muddy land that is left uncovered when the sea goes out at low tide

pod a group of cetaceans that live together

predator an animal that hunts and eats other animals

prey an animal that is killed by another animal for food

species a group of living things that look similar and can mate

tropical the area near the equator where the water is warm all year

wetlands land that is partly covered by water, such as swamps and marshes

wingspan the distance across a bird's wings, measured from wingtip to wingtip

zooplankton tiny animals, eggs, and larvae that drift through the water

Read More

Lavender, Julie and David. *Seal (Spotlight on Nature).* Mankato, MN: Creative Education and Creative Paperback, 2025.

Nakaya, Andrea C. *Healthy Oceans: Why They Matter.* San Diego: ReferencePoint Press, Inc., 2023.

Nickum, Nora. *Superpod: Saving the Endangered Orcas of the Pacific Northwest.* Chicago: Chicago Review Press, 2023.

O'Dowd, Della. *Sea Otters in Their Ecosystems (Vital to Earth! Keystone Species Explained).* Minneapolis: Bearport Publishing Company, 2024.

Learn More Online

1. Go to **FactSurfer.com** or scan the QR code below.
2. Enter "**Marine Mammals & Seabirds**" into the search box.
3. Click on the cover of this book to see a list of websites.

Index

albatross 7, 14–15
avocets 9
blubber 22, 26, 28
camouflage 9
cetaceans 38
cormorants 16
crustaceans 4–5, 10–11, 15, 18–20, 26, 38, 41
dolphins 24–25, 38, 40–41
ducks 18–19
dugong 24, 36
eagles 7
eggs 6, 12–13, 20, 22–23, 35
frigatebirds 16–17
global warming 29, 32, 35
guillemots 20
gulls 12
krill 5, 22, 39, 41
lobsters 31
manatees 24, 36–37
mangrove forests 10
mating 17, 20–21, 28, 36
mollusks 8, 18–19, 26–27
mussels 8
nests 11, 13, 15–16, 19–20, 23
octopuses 23, 31, 41
orcas 29, 40
otters 24, 26–27
penguins 22–23, 43
petrels 14
plankton 4–5
plants 18, 36–37
polar bears 4, 24, 29, 34
porpoises 24, 38, 40
puffins 20
seagrass 4, 36–37
sea lions 24, 32–33
seals 24, 28, 30–35
shrimp 9, 11, 29
skimmers 12
skuas 12
spoonbills 10
squid 4, 16, 22–23, 32, 41
walruses 28–29
whales 4–5, 24–25, 35, 38, 40